M
is for
MOTORCYCLE

Written by Kim Faganello
Illustrated by Keilan Faganello

 is for Armor

be safe when you ride!

B is for Boots

where your feet fit inside.

D is for Dualsport

↑
DUALSPORT

that makes a **BRAP** sound.

E is for Engine

that spins the back tire.

F is for Foot pegs

that

help

you

get

higher!

FOOTPEGS

G is for Gauges

that show us our speed.

I

is for Incline

that goes up up up up.

J

is for Jumps that go

BUMP

BUMP

BUMP

K is for Kickstand

that holds bikes upright.

M is for Motorcycle

in all sizes and shapes.

N is for Numbers

that go on these plates.

O is for Oil that goes in right here.

P is for Piston

that powers the gears.

Q is for Quickly get over that log!

R is for Revving

so your engine won't bog.

S is for Shocks

that keep the ride smooth.

T is for Tires

that grip so you'll move.

U is for Under

a low mossy trèe.

W is for Wheelies

when you ride on the rear.

 is for X Games,

held once a year.

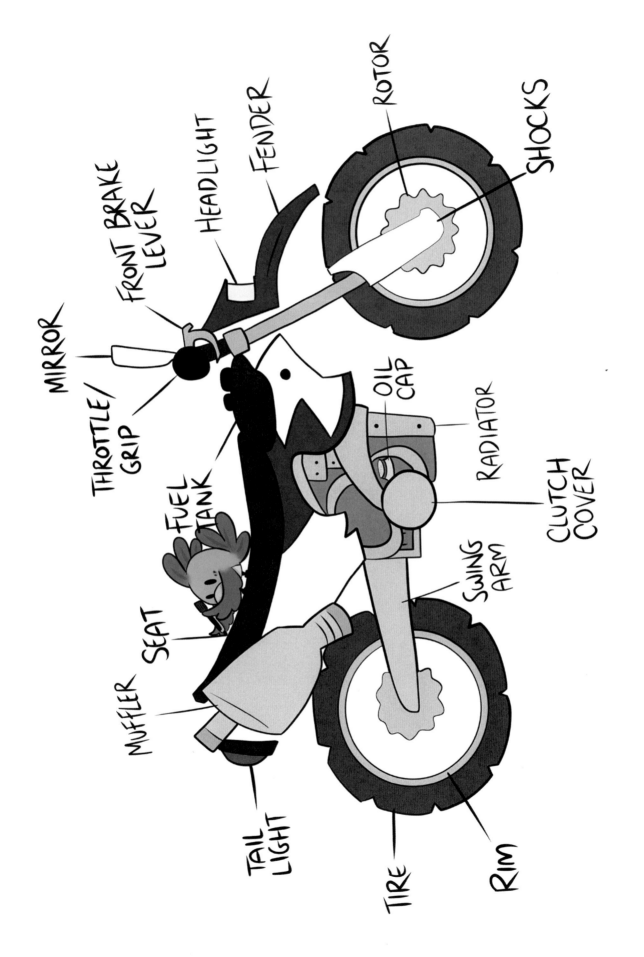

About KIMKEY

Kim is a Youtube Motovlogger from Victoria, BC, Canada. Using his experiences of being a husband and father of three, he began writing childrens' books that he would have enjoyed reading to his boys when they were little.

 youtube.com/RideVictoria

KEILAN HAS BEEN CARTOONING SINCE HE WAS OLD ENOUGH TO HOLD A PENCIL. HE WRITES, DRAWS AND ANIMATES AS A HOBBY ARTIST. ALTHOUGH HE WAS BORN IN VICTORIA, BC, CANADA, KEILAN CONSIDERS JAPAN A SECOND HOME. CURRENTLY, HE RESIDES IN HONOLULU, HAWAII.

 youtube.com/Keilanify

CONNECT WITH US!

facebook.com/KimKeyBooks

KimKey Books

KimKeyBooks@gmail.com